Jonah's Promise

Jonah's Promise

poems by
Adam Sol

Mid-List Press
Minneapolis

F I R S T   S E R I E S :   P O E T R Y

Published by Mid-List Press
4324 12th Avenue South
Minneapolis, Minnesota 55407-3218
Website: www.midlist.org

Manufactured in the United States of America

First printing: July 2000

Library of Congress Cataloging-in-Publication Data
Sol, Adam, 1969-
    Jonah's promise : poems / by Adam Sol.
        p. cm.
    "First series: poetry."
    ISBN 0-922811-47-4 (alk. paper)
     1. Jews—United States—Poetry. 2. Judaism—Poetry. I. Title.
PS3569.O46 J66 2000
811'.6—dc21   00-040209

Contents

If there's nothing on the earth worthwhile, we have to pretend there is.
—Sidney Nyburg

Jonah's Promise

I'm supposed to sit with the coffin for an hour and read Psalms.
Shout unto the Lord all the earth. Serve the Lord with gladness.

Upstairs in the funeral home, well-dressed men make arrangements
amid electric lanterns flickering, a candlelight effect.

In a back room, gorgeous dark wood caskets are displayed
like bunkbeds, neat price cards placed near the heads.

Marcus is waiting in the basement, encased in white pine. I relieve a couple
who look up, spooked, as if I'd walked in on them dressing.

They lend me their bible and rush off to work, pointing
to where they had left off. A state-mandated

workers' rights notice blares minimum wage at the opposite wall.

•

The basement is damp but warm, despite the snow outside
and the old windows, dusty with rust and chipped paint.

Extra coffins, wrapped in plastic tarps, are piled against the wall
behind the water heater. A plumber weaves behind the pipes,

discretely winding valves. *It is a good thing to give thanks unto the Lord,*
and to sing praises unto Thy name. I've always hated Psalms,

their open-armed belief. As if David, or whoever wrote them,
didn't spend most of his time fighting or running for his life.

But tradition holds them the best way to comfort the dead.
Maybe for their steadiness, the reassuring drone. I read one

in half-voice while the plumber cranks something together.
Who needs it.

I start flipping pages, figuring Marcus won't mind. Land on Jonah.
His prayer in the whale: *But I will sacrifice unto Thee*

with the voice of thanksgiving; that which I have vowed I will pay.
Okay, okay, I will do as you say. I'd promise too if I were swimming

in some grouper's abdomen. Even still, after the vomiting,
when he finally gets to Nineveh,

his prophecy is the shortest and lamest in the whole bible:
Yet forty days and Nineveh shall be overthrown.

Five words in the Hebrew.
It's as if being ignored is what he'd wanted, to be mocked or stoned,

and then to rise triumphant and forgiving like Isaiah,
or some AM radio preacher summoning the End of Days.

But Nineveh *believes*. His grudging mumblings are heard
and *presto!*, the city is fasting, man and beast, the king himself

scraping skin off his knees in a pool of ash and pebbles.
Jonah's half-assed efforts trebly fulfilled, and Jonah left outside the city,

hungry for blood like a late-night cable tv addict,
the only words he has spoken proven false. The prophecy refutes itself.

•

One of the home's functionaries quietly interrupts:
Is there anything I need? More light? No thanks.

I'm supposed to be reading out loud, I guess.
That's why he came up to me. Not doing my duty.

Was this not my saying, when I was yet in mine own country?
Therefore I fled unto Tarshish, for I knew Thou art a gracious God,

compassionate, long-suffering, abundant in mercy, and repentest Thee of evil.
Well then, why the prayer in the whale, hotshot?

If you knew you'd be used, why repent? I flip back the page:
That which I have vowed I will pay. What did you vow?

You didn't promise anything. What do you owe them?
I don't have to be sitting here. I didn't even know the guy.

Asshole asks me if I need more light.
I am not Jonah. I came when I was called.

•

What gets me is how he takes it. Jonah knows that God
is going to make a complete idiot out of him.

The morning noise of the city rises to his ears
like a laughing rebuke: Go, do this for Me, after all

your protests and revisions, go
and I will make you My fool, to the great relief of all.

He knows all this is going to happen, he says so,
and still he does it.

I will wrangle with Your mercy.
I will complain of Your tenderness.

Yet will I do these things.
What else is there for me?

•

I am startled when my relief thumps down the stairs in heels:
a woman my wife knows.

Marcus accepts the switch without comment, and I show her
where I'd left off Psalms. *Read whatever you want,* I tell her.

She sits and starts before I've left the room,
calmly, as though she sits sh'mira every week.

I climb the stairs
and reappear in the living world as she starts

a psalm of David. *I will sing of mercy and justice.*
Unto you will I sing praises.

Doctrine

Sundays I sit on the floor in a paper
sandbox, distorted like a Venus landscape,
its edges leaning up in the heat.
In a few hours I'm scratching my face
and sick of myself for not doing anything.
I suppose it's the same for everybody.
Instead of getting in the car and heading
wherever to start the great something,
I take a shower, gorge myself on leftovers,
stare. Good days
I get some work done, you know how it is.
Indifferent days it doesn't much matter
that nothing gets done. A woman
from here went missing
around Christmas. Story goes
she bashed her car into a tree,
lost her grip on the wheel,
was last seen running. I admit
I don't understand. I have no
reason to kill myself. I read the paper.
People doing things to each other in countries
I'll never visit. I return to certain
places over and over, leave
the rest alone. Like questions.
On the highway through Crescent City,
on a road trip that carried me comfortably
from friend to friend, I saw a deer
on the shoulder. It was kicking wildly
but with that stoic deer face.
I hope it died by daybreak.
I hope you can see what I'm saying.
I paid for my room that night
and slept. I didn't call the police,
the animal shelter, the park ranger,
my mother. I slept well, woke up early
and started for Seattle.

Life, McKenzie

This is the envelope, my gap-toothed friend.
A week before your wedding, you were with Hudson, thumbing your players into place,
and suddenly the chaotic music, the headwreck.
The screen goes ebullient blank: you've been sacked. You can't get through it.

Northward glares the gaping airport, escape, the seedy excursion.
Another winsome undergrad to spill your brilliance over.
And Monday? What will happen Monday?
Will there be a Monday?

Don't do it. You are tight-lipped as a Kirts ravioli,
but I know about you.
I was with you on the roof blowing smoke at the telephone wires.
I was in the gutter picking up pins.
I held your hand on Terry's knee. Your excuses are stupid,
but it's not reason enough to put yourself to sleep.
Even with the news, your fiancée's
been tinting the windows for you, as she promised.

Listen to me.
Let the limousines yawn in the morning.
Let the dumb doves dive into windows,
and your Maura murals frown down from the walls.
Let Dick clang out his sorry songs of stone and mercurochrome.
What do they know?

You've got sweet elephant ears to look forward to.
And the fanfare, the ridiculous radicchio,
the in-laws and crazed caterers gathering on the Columbus horizon like a
    swarm of wasps—
Isn't it a glorious, hysterical music?
Don't kill yourself, you asshole.
Let them make for you a new exasperation.

"Blessed Is the One Who Releases Me from This Responsibility"

The girl's over-rehearsed. Her rushed rendition of the prayers

is a toneless slur, and she blushes an angry maroon
at the inept banter of the new rabbi, his sweet bumbling efforts

to present her with candlesticks "on behalf of the whole congregation."
We're so proud. Grandma grins shrilly, owning the room.

Afterwards, with the hors d'oeuvre band playing antiseptic swank,
you joke with the Latino bartender strangling in his bowtie.

Show him you're not like the rest of them. Give a knowing nod
to the drop-dead dropout serving the stuffed mushrooms.

You both know how plastic it is: the blasted hair of the aunts,
the portly confidence of the uncles, the toothpicks

and square napkins damp with chicken fat and teriyaki sauce,
the cantaloupe castles and shimmering Pegasus ice sculpture.

The girl enters the hall amid a clutch of conspirators,
their shoulders hunched, metal-clad teeth hidden by hands,

nails bitten down and painted over. A boy in khaki slacks and navy jacket
leans by the door—a prepubescent Jimmy Deanstein.

Now the deejay's invocation: *A round of applause everybody
for the people who made this all possible.*

Mother, in her second outfit, is just glad it's almost over.
Father's pocketing envelopes by the dozen. And you,

with your glass of flat champagne, your potatoes and salmon
languishing in their respective sauces, what are you muttering about?

Don't you dance with Auntie Beatie through her cloud of Tanqueray?
Don't you sample the birthday cake with its pasty sugar flowers?

How dare you? They're your family.
The rowdy spectacle is not why you're here. You *belong* here.

You are stuck to this as surely as the syrup on your tie.
And that shamed sneer on your lip: give it a name. Give it your own.

Oral Palliative

Even after the burned hat, the shattered broom,
he's still content to kiss babies at the bistro,
and nonchalantly greet the passers-by.
It's enough to burn the enamel from your teeth.

My dear angry friend, waiting on wicker for some
change of events, watching grackles go at it on the gravel.
They find nourishment everywhere, the scamps.
Unlike you who, with thinning clavicle
and dirty breakfast smoke in your hair,
can't separate carbohydrates from lipids,
not even with a hatchet. What can you do?
Especially with the grainy television
telling you it's *you*—your clogged pores, your persistent yeast.
Oh, how you sit like a solitary city
now that your rodent prince has run off. Sister,

I am no one you should listen to.
I have my suspect motivations.
But I've seen the vague shrug,
the broken brick, and such. Trust me on this one score:
your mouth has powers he can't contend with,
and all his bastard bearded grinning
can't alter an adverb.
Let your scar stories be your best batter.

Poem

I am trying to find a parking space—
sweat gathers on my lower back.
Something rattles from lack of oil.

No, I'm shaving my arms with a dry razor.
I'm feeling pent up like an olive,
bloated and green, clogged with something
that only half belongs to me.

Or I'm making a decision
in a house on stilts
that will alter everything.

We are doomed to experience our heavens.

Maybe ketchup is burning in the toaster oven,
my English muffin pizza searing in the coils.
Maybe I'm pouring my heart
into a martini glass.

It could be anything: catapult, curling iron,
footsteps overhead that make the ceiling creak.

Today I saw a woman who reminded me of you
and she might as well have been you—
we would have meant roughly
the same to each other.
She was wearing your jeans
and you were embracing her father,
telling him your secrets,
lifting your shirt to show him

the scar on your back. Lover, stranger,
we are as close as this page is to your face
and that's not nearly enough.

Assurances

The soda cans you bag in bins
work their way to factories and are
remade as soda cans.

The ozone layer will continue
to protect us from the sun. You must

have faith that things
will go roughly as expected:

that the ink in your jeans will not poison you,
that your lungs won't collapse,
that the car swerving into your lane

will respond to your horn.
In all, there's a lot that can go wrong.

Look at the burst bulb at your desk.
Look at the newspaper
and the crazy hemorrhages in the neighborhood.

You should know, living so close to the hospital,
it takes nothing to break the night with sirens.

Still, you must believe in things.

In truth and justice, for instance,
despite all evidence to the contrary.
You must believe your hand
will do what you ask, within reason.
You must smile at people you know
and assume they remember you fondly.
You must breathe, and hope for the best.
Alternatives are reasonable but not worth mentioning.

And when something finally does happen—
when you are struck on your bike by an errant brick,

when your mother is on the crashed airplane,
when your husband comes home smelling of musk,

you must be surprised.
Say: I never thought it would happen to me.
This will calm the others.

Forbidding Mourning

—for A.L.

In this light, at the window, her reflection
　　　finally looks as thin to her
as everyone's been saying. Her wrist
　　　is tired of supporting her head,

her nose tissue-sore, her eyes
　　　dry as ash. It's going to be another
goddamned beautiful day: white light
　　　on the dogwood makes everything . . .

Never mind. The garbageman comes.
　　　She should take out the garbage.
She hates the man with the thick glove
　　　on one hand, his forearms glistening.

She hates him for being a garbageman—
　　　for working, even whistling,
today, while she sits, unable
　　　to do anything but stare.

Shouldn't the air be full of grief?
　　　Couldn't the processes of the world—
for one day—cease?
　　　Shouldn't he know somehow?

Of course not. And if she decides
　　　to smash her hand through the window—
as she half-believes she will do—
　　　if she spends seven days howling,

or if she goes into the kitchen,
　　　lifts out the white bag,
absurdly sterile, ties it shut
　　　and carries it to the man outside—

a week from now he will come again,
    as scheduled, faithful as a compass.
It's enough to make her grief as thin
    as paper, and as precious.

Song

I'm thinking of things we can't do.
Thin ice. Friends' lovers.
You want to drink from the cold river
washing over stones,
but you know the factories; you want
to swim but it's five below.
Wet paint. Porcelain.
Barbed wire fences with gaps
large enough to tempt our hands,
bleeding knuckles, tongue on lip.
Mary, he doesn't own you. Stay.

Mouthful of Sand

I gave up on words when my daughter died.
    What use? They deceive.
       They lisp. I stopped
greeting people in the hallway.
     I pointed at pastries in the hospital cafeteria.
     I looked at signs but refused
to read them. I kept Mahler and Matisse but gave up Keats.

•

I am poured out like water,
    And all my bones are out of joint;

My strength is dried up like a potsherd;
    And my tongue cleaveth to my throat.

•

Holly would answer the phone and cry
until her words were garbled and unintelligible.
I would hold her from behind, trying

to be steadfast and mute, like our house.
I could hear through the receiver people saying,
"I'm so sorry," or "Feel better." Words.

In the living room, the tv on but muted,
the two of us curled in a quilt,
knees up, feet on the coffee table.

•

When Holly was pregnant, I would talk her to sleep,
    making up stories about the child.

I'd invent piano recitals, car trips to the mountains,
    a word for the smell of her hair.

She said my voice soothed her. I think it was only
      because of how deep it is and how,

when she rested her head on my chest, she heard the words
      before they left my mouth.

•

The nurse urged us to name her,

            to help us grieve. We had to decide
if we should use the name we'd wanted for her,

            my mother's name,
or if we should save it for another child.

            When Holly gave her to me,
I didn't know where to put my hands.

•

Pamphlet: *Begin*

with small tasks first,
such as cooking,

laundry, cleaning.
When you're ready,

gradually move
up to more

difficult matters.
You'll be surprised at what

you are able to do.

•

She said, *David, this isn't right,* and my answer

was, *Don't worry. I'll talk you through it.*

Cramp in her back, spot of blood on the car seat,

and a year's crescendo dispersed three months early,

like soot, like dandelion spores, like

·

Like nothing. It's like absolutely nothing in the world.

·

At the mall, I hold her hand
amid the wave of shouts,
the urgings and petitions,

gawky teenagers in polyester caps
intoning, "Can I help you?"
Can you help me.

Later, rain in the parking lot.
White shine of the lamps, wet
reflections on the roofs of cars.
Holly waiting under the awning.

I have no idea where we are.
Syllables of rain batter my head,
seep under my sweater and down
my back. Cold water in my shoes.

·

What shall I liken to thee,
    O daughter of Jerusalem?

What shall I equal to thee,
    that I may comfort thee?

•

I finally discover our dumpy sedan behind a pickup,

and tear back to Holly, skidding the tires.
She is sitting on the sidewalk,
head on her knees, a lower-case 'a.'

Her smile through the window
while I reach across to unlock the door,
and the damp smell of her jacket.

Then they come back. I open my cracked lips
and the words come tumbling out of my mouth
like water from a burst balloon:

every stupid crypto-messenger,
every useless palliative, every apology,
every 'if,' every 'why,' every 'we.'

She lets out a breath, the first word
in a new language only the two of us know.

Burying Carnations

Windy days in Missouri, Rosemary
wanders in the orchard. Fourteen,
the cold fading out, she's waiting

for what she's been told comes next.
Sometimes in the winter, carnations
bloom in her bedroom,

gifts from boys in her class who
can't seem to remember their own names.
They grin at the window.

Before they fade,
Rosemary wraps them in tissue
and buries them in the orchard.

She hopes to find them in spring,
but they are like gypsies: once turned out,
they rarely return.

Rosemary slips the hair out of her mouth
with a finger. The air is ripe with apples.
She stands on her toes to reach one,

holds it, pulls until the whole tree
quiets. The green rough thing is
smaller than her fist, and stronger.

She lets it go, and the orchard rests.
There will be plenty of apples.
Today she is looking for flowers.

Bris

The strap from the Pentax circles Allen's forearm
    like t'fillin. Two video
cameras roll while the grandfather sits down, white as gauze.
    The moyl offers the baby
cloth soaked in schnapps, then performs the ceremony.
    The cry is the sound
of stone cracking. Thirty men shuffle beneath tallitot: another son
    permanently altered,
"entered into the covenant," the verb strangely passive.
    Through the lattice of the mechitza,
we can see the mother, still ashen, and the others on their toes.
    One davens in the back,
her hair coming out of the bun, face serious and defiant.

    My father and I, Reform cousins—
awkward in our kipot, without prayerbooks—grin at each other
    as if that could save us, and in a way,
it does. Allen puts down the camera to hug us hello. Everyone
    is greeting each other, answering
the mourners' kaddish reflexively, a reassuring drone.
    Then the child is returned to his mother,
and we move downstairs for bagels and whitefish as only
    Teaneck can provide. The mother's
black-hatted, bearded brother tickles one of his seven children
    on the stairway. We don't
exchange remarks with him, and he eyes us with something
    akin to suspicion. He knows
who we aren't. His hat leans back on his head like it's
    too small for him.

The father gives a drash, explaining the newborn's name.
    It's the first anyone's heard it—
Gavriel, for the mother's grandfather, dead only a year.
    He invokes Elijah—when the prophet
failed to stop the Israelites from worshipping idols,
    he walked to Sinai and begged God
to take his life. "It is hopeless, a waste, a lost cause."

God rebuked him saying, "You are wrong,
and I will curse you in this way. Whenever Jews celebrate
    Passover or perform a bris,
they will invoke your name to remind you how wrong you were."
    And it's done. We are dismissed
to our brunches. Aunt Holly's hat matches the tablecloth.

    Silent, Gavriel winces
at his grandmother's shoulder while she spreads lox on a bagel.
    The father scurries about,
dispensing prayerbooks: "We're benching in a few minutes."
    We exchange bris stories—
the aunt who fainted, the moyl who distributed his calling card
    after the ceremony, advertising
his handiwork. We slip out when the chanting begins.
    My father and I take our
kipot off in the coat room, leave them on the shelf
    where we found them.
We are free to resume our status as anonymous commuters
    crossing the GW Bridge.
Instead we are newly enmeshed. We leave the small synagogue
    quiet, the closed door
blocking all sound of celebration, the morning stripped
    of its haze, sharp and cold.
We squint to hide the raw flesh of our eyes.

Variations on *Jonah*

1.

Ragged, he chuckles in the dank of his overturned ship,
picking splinters out of what used to be the ceiling.
The clouds must have broken: even through the pitch and tar
sealing the hull, he can see bright patches.
He has all the fruit he can eat. Three rats aboard
seem content to feast on the port side and leave starboard for him.
He considers praying in thanks for his salvation,
but thinks better of it, not sure what might hear.
Escape is a room with no windows.
He thinks to himself, *I am free.*
The storm is over, the sea quiet, and I am a man with a mouth
and hands to feed it with. The oranges are sweet.
He peels another, spits the seeds down the hatch into the water.
May they sprout water-oranges. I will harvest them with the shankbones of sailors.

2.

Every Thursday someone comes to harangue us.
Usually it's about the hungry,
or our daughters, but there was this one punk
who had us in ashes for two full weeks.
We had a time.
He stank like the rest,
but he didn't shout or wave his arms.
Not even the eye-rolling and slaver
that got us last season. But you know
how the aside sometimes grabs you
more than singing—*Oh, by the way,*
for lunch I ate your dog.
His timing was impeccable. I don't exactly
remember what he said, but the deadpan delivery,
the easy slouch—he changed the form overnight.
We would have made him King
for the Summer Festival,
but he insisted on camping in the hills.
Let the artist live his life, I guess.
He might have pulled it off again
if it hadn't been for the wars,
which always make us look to the traditional ways.

3.

When they threw me over,
like some apple core or rotted sack of meal,
I'd scarcely lost my breath before the sun broke through.
I could almost have swum back to them
if it hadn't been for my legs, which were so tired,
and my shoulders, which ached from holding the rails.
Down it was dark, but the light
punched through the waves in small squares,
like headless glowing fish. I reached a hand out
but it was too far, and then
there was the other fish, the great one. In the end
it wasn't the drowning
or the time inside that made me change my mind.
It was the swallowing,
feeling myself and everything around me—debris from the cargo,
ropes of kelp—sucked in, just as if I were falling,
but knowing exactly where I'd land. There was
nothing to do—I let every muscle go slack.

4.

The last part came first.
I was sitting outside the city at the family tombs,
thinking of my fortunes
and feeling strong and happy in the shade of a cedar.
Then it began to rain, as if
to defy my glory, and I laughed at God's joke:
what else can you do? That's when it hit me.
What else *could* one do? Resist, defy, of course,
but look where that got Aaron's sons.
There's plenty of arguing and negotiations
by patriarch and prophet, but you always know
those guys will buckle eventually. I wanted someone
who'd spit to the very end.
The whale stuff came after a few revisions.
The editors shredded it, of course—took out
the love story, the parable of the broken wheel—
but they paid well enough,
and one even deigned to marry my daughter.

Gull House

—South Kingston, R.I.

Those stilts have held their own
against the sea and wind
for thirty years—

nobody builds so close
to the water any more.
Last month's nor'easter

tore the staircase clean off
and disemboweled the plumbing.
Now the concrete base

hangs four feet off the sand,
a great over-full udder.
I almost expect it to tilt,

or maybe the middle will suddenly
collapse, like a soufflé.
One hollow concrete square—

I can't even tell
if it's from the house—
lies half-buried in the sand.

It would make a perfect
hiding place, except
there's nowhere else to look.

Every once in a while
the local realtor drives up,
trailing the Tom's Electric van

or a plumber's pickup,
to estimate. The owner
has fled to Florida.

Meanwhile, a host of gulls
ignore us from the roof.
Lately they've been playing

with the weathervane—they flirt
and fight, riding the wind
that makes the thing spin.

The perch provides them with
a perfect view of the water
from Narragansett, past

the tourist beaches, out
to the Charlestown breachway.
On a clear day like today,

the birds look proud there.
They squint at the wind
like old adventurers,

dismissive and nostalgic.
Whatever they see with their harsh,
yellow eyes, they own.

The Merry Crew

The boiler boys below decks
are rife with pox
and the captain's head has changed
to a mantis'.

We are skirting a storm
that has claimed the lives
of our radio personalities.

The first mate
has given us permission
to contemplate our lonelinesses.
They are perfect as tuning forks.

We tighten the rigging. Do not despair,
the first mate says. Tlik, klik,
says the captain.

We hum the song
of the broken mast
and hold our voices
tight to our bellies

because there is no water
and the starboard curtain
of rain
has twisted into brambles.
We are a merry crew—

our ship rocks
in our neighborhood indentation.

The surfaces around us
are anxious to turn
inside themselves,
and we won't disappoint them.

We burn the salt soup
and stash shoelaces
in secret places. We eat

the sea with brio.
We piss blood, we claw
hearts into wood,
we gain altitude.

At our last port,
a dead man in a stone raft
set course against the wind.

Thrash

fifteen minutes of the backstreet downbeat syncopated terrorism coming off
the main stage firebrand suburb boys going dirty you can feel it coming on
and some jerk in the back nursing his Beck's like Mac Davis   people's
sweat in the air flying up like sparks with the light and you're in the middle
your fists on some guy's sweaty t-shirt no way out no way closer you're
getting crushed and starting to think it's groovy   security meatheads push
the crowd down and the noise and the heat and this as alive as you get
otherwise you outside playing Dagwood to the big man, outside you
punching computer timecards, outside you e-mailing what's left of your old
gang making marriage out of molehills last vestiges of premonitions and
hope in the world   guitar kid is turning on the wah-wah singer's whirling
dervish and all you see behind the drum's a spray of hair, red in the light,
gold in the light, turning maniacal circles, centerpiece ringmaster, the one
guy in the room who really gets to hit something   and you think, this
world is going to shit but not me I'm not going with it I'm gonna blow
through the air like a gun

Our Business is Rejoicing

Between channels, brief snarls of static: commercials for massacre.
Fess up to your ambition, the smile says. You want this car.
The sleek black creature arcs around a tight curve near an ocean,
the only sound a cello's arpeggio.
Cue makeup, bogus night lighting. Bring on the fury of insect repellent.

Quick blip and three thousand young bodies reach for me in baseball caps,
shoulders burnt blue in the faulty color of my old screen.
See how it's done? How the bright ball lights up the world?
Now the trussed-up family of articulate professionals solves a quick crisis
    with a heart-to-heart.
See the love in the three-walled room? Make the snake retract.
No. Make him eat his rattle.

Stalin loved Shostakovich's Fifth Symphony, the glorious hysterical finale,
    braying trumpets, brash ridiculous cymbals.
Triumph over trial, or so he thought it. The composer's suitcase packed
    beneath his bed.
It is as if someone were beating you with a stick saying, 'Your business is rejoicing,
your business is rejoicing,' and you rise, shaky,
and go marching off, muttering, 'Our business is rejoicing.'

Restate in unison.
Timpani for canned laughter, trombone for the dazed look of new fame.
The faint electric screech inside the house like tremolo violins.

Document

Page of dead letters. Dead words
in a dead language for a dead man's wife.
To be granted release from her marriage,
she must prove her husband dead—
witnesses, tokens, last words. To give
a death to the missing man, Jewish Pole
conscripted into the Russian Army,
the Eastern front a growing place for wires.

Thirty months after his letters stop coming,
a one-legged man from thirty miles away
arrives saying he will sign the document for her,
if someone who can write
will take his story down. It is sealed, made legal,
by the rabbi in Lublin. She will carry
it with her to the States with her son,
Abe. She will remarry.

> *I met Jacob Sol when we first entered*
> *the Army. He was a printer from Lublin.*
> *He had red hair and brown eyes. He was*
> *not very tall. On the 29th of December, 1914,*
> *I believe near the town of D—*
> *our regiment was shelled by a German force.*
> *We all ducked behind a wooden barrier.*
> *When the shelling was over, Jacob did not get up.*

We weren't sure the name wasn't shortened
at Ellis Island until our grandmother found this:
Yiddish scribble my sister holds.
Her Linguistics professor translated it for us:
"printer?" "scribe?" The handwriting is faint
and the idioms obscure, buried in Polish markings,
stamps and creases like his corpse somewhere underground.
But the name, *Sol,* is clear and sharp as blood on glass.

Jew in a New Suit

—for Abe Sol (1914-1986)

(Ice Man)

There he goes, the old man selling ice,
       and my old man's old man following close behind,

pursuing the dying tradesman
of a dying trade.

Sorry, we got a Frigidaire.

    Down Houston some bum
is kicking a dog away from a herring skeleton.

Get yerself outa Manhattan,
        immigrant boy,
    Jew-kid, shaker, brakeman, brain.

                    •

"Dear Helen,
    I'm sorry I can't come out to see you in Williamsburg
this weekend—I don't have a dime for the trolley.
I would have called but I didn't have a nickel . . ."

                    •

(1944—First Cavalry)

MacArthur estimated we'd lose a million men,

and they're waiting on the *Franklin,* ankles around the saddle,
when the news comes that by some miracle of thermonucleation
    they're just going to walk into Tokyo for breakfast.

This is how you say Hello.
This is how you say I'm sorry for your uncle.

●

Look at him now,
    Jew in the new suit.

Watch him work, watch him
    putting on his new hat and coat.

Watch the corner boys resent him with cement.

He's on his way to the top,
and his boys play stickball with the best of 'em.
He's putting in his time at Madison's Used Cars,
    doing the books for an old crook,

        watching the clock.

●

How a Jew's money moves:
Houston Street,
Williamsburg, Brooklyn,
Forest Hills, Queens,
East Brunswick, New Jersey,
Connecticut, Connecticut, Connecticut—
        sound of billfolds slapping shut,

      refuge, symbol, pinnacle.

    Contemporary with grass, septic tank, private well,

and the grandson playing soldier in the woods.

●

(1974)

Cement back patio of a California beach hotel,
my father is taking us out for ice cream.

The old man sits up from the sweaty plastic deck chair,
pale khaki Bermuda shorts belted tight.

The shrugged question:
both hands out, eyebrows up, slight nod. My father

puts out his hand, shakes his head no,
explains: *He's asking if I need any money.*

•

Now the old man's disease has shrunk his brain to a raisin.
The Citation spins,
    struck handily by Long Island girls after the wedding.

I'm waiting at the hospital like I'm waiting for a bus.

I'm doing my best not to cringe at the growing horror
behind those eyes that once . . .
Grandma wipes his mouth with an old handkerchief.

Even his death is timed for my convenience,
after I get back from a trip to the beach.

Grandpa, I am reaping what you've sown.
It's your sweet fruit in my bitter mouth.

My Father's Hands

It's a school night. While I get ready for bed,
downstairs my father plays the Bach fugue
he always messes up near the end.
He reworks the phrase, gets through,
does it again. Practicing. For years
I will believe this piece has a repeating coda.
Because I have started my own lessons
I pay special attention while I undress.
Listen for one of my new words: crescendo.
Feel the speed of his fingers
in my own awkward hands as they lift
the blue blanket from my bed.
It's before we've moved, before
we've found ourselves in a Connecticut contemporary
twice the size of my father's ambitions.
Maybe while he plays he considers
mortgages, moving companies, schools.
Maybe he is frustrated by how his fingers
have forgotten the tricky trill at the end,
how he must repeat himself.
He has not played much lately.
And like any eight-year-old,
I am oblivious. I think I am waiting
for him to finish so I can sleep. Of course
I am out in moments, and the fugue turns itself
into a nocturne. I dream in E flat major,
my father's hands
raising me like a glass of wine.

The Sacred and The Profane

We sit in a circle while our leader, a senior,
plays sentimental melodies on guitar. *Blessed are You,*
who separates light from darkness. He's having a thing

with the Vernon girl whose brother dropped out of Dartmouth.
We've seen her sputtering into the phone after hours.
Our leader is less than competent. He watches his fingers on the neck

as if they were someone else's hands, and the muted strings buzz.
We respond with harmonic whispers. We are
the NorthEast Federation of Temple Youth, on a weekend retreat,

and we have spent all day eyeing each other
during discussion groups, lectures and slide shows,
waiting for this service and the dance which follows. *The Sabbath*

from the six ordinary days of the week. Teens and Torah, scripture and sex.
The Jews of the greater Hartford area sleep soundly tonight,
knowing their children are renewing tradition,

learning prayers their grandparents would be proud to hear.
All for less than the price of a ski trip.
The House of Israel from all other peoples.

Havdalah ends the Sabbath, ends our programming for the weekend,
breaks the spell. The braided candle, bent from use,
crackles and winks out in a pewter glass of syrupy wine.

Closing song, then we are released. Down the hall, the music starts
with Madonna, then eerily works its way into Prince:
Dearly beloved, we are gathered here today to get through this thing called life.

Our ankles are numb from sitting cross-legged on the floor,
our eyes still adjusting to the colored light.
The holy from the ordinary. The DJ, in a sequined purple shirt

and Miami sportjacket, growls into the mike.
We lean on his table, careful not to disturb the console,
and make petitions, some of which he grants, RayBans glittering.

Against Nostalgia

Nothing is more boring than my own life.
    I'm not going to spout elegies about

the trail I used to walk to school, back in the rural
    suburbs of Connecticut—lush,

ridiculous and expensive. There are other worlds.
    And you can't know that trail now

because it's been paved over to make room
    for Suncrest Drive, with its

million-dollar yards. If you know other trails
    like it, with their

horseflies, tree roots and spider web strands
    conspiring against you,

blackberry bushes stretching across for light, you can
    keep it to yourself.

Old, lived-in New England: tobacco farmers
    cleared the land of trees and Pequots,

made their little whirlpool in history, then sold
    the farms to New Yorkers

who let the trees reassert themselves. So the spot
    behind the backstop

where I lost my class ring sliding down the mud,
    is irrelevant. Same with

the stubborn stream alive with salamanders, tadpoles
    and rusted Pepsi cans where

Jason Holterman—whose National Socialist grandfather
    fled New York in 1941—

offered me hash before I'd even heard the word.
    So what if there's a meadow

where Laurie Slaymaker and I used to meet with her
    sleeping bag, hot

clear nights of the summer, mosquito bites on my thighs?
    It's also where commuters

fled income taxes and established an American royalty
    built on the Puritan belief

that good fortune reflects good character. You've seen
    the movies. And if

you were quiet on the way to school early in the morning,
    you could spy a deer—

deer grown so populous from want of wolves they push
    each other into traffic—

grazing on maple saplings,
    the moment of grace
        when she heard you and turned—.

Now we're clearing out again, heading south and west.
    Taxes stayed low

but nothing else did, and the city keeps creeping closer.
    Smell of rotting wood,

scolding squirrels, shelf mushrooms, sweat gathering
    on my back beneath my pack,

and stone fences all around, even in the deepest thickets.
    It's like any childhood

landscape, and even then I never got the feeling I was
    alone, just that I'd temporarily

escaped notice. I get the same feeling now on the subway.
    So why think about the way

the light would filter down green through the leaves
    of sugar maples and red oak

to isolate stones on the trail, so that they seemed
    to point my way for me

back when I was so young and impressionable?

Now, When

Outside, the granite field, ringed
by rusted wire and felled maples.
Metal flakes flicker on boulders,
and beetles teem in the wet wood.

My house is crammed with windows, windows
on other worlds, windows on breakdown.
Deer choke on my tomatoes.
Lice on the deer suck deer blood. And I,

I eat the lice. In my gut, the tomato dissolves,
reconstructs itself as motion,
an absent-minded gesture of the hand.

What I've learned of cell biology
confirms it: we are precariously constructed,
paper cranes on a hot air balloon.

If all these bodies, these words,
are only proteins strung together, and the proteins
are only carbons, and the carbons mostly space,
how can we touch water without dissolving?

In the yard, a robin bounds around,
knowing what he wants.

Vienna March

Boys in uniform call from a bridge above,
but you don't speak their language.
Stop yourself from turning. If you lean down,
sidelocks shield your face. Gulls
patrol the Danube. You are warm in your black coat.

On the wall, a graffiti canvas: P +
G, Hüsker Dü. The headless stick figures,
swastikas. There are dozens.
You've seen them before: pinwheels

etched into phone booths, elevator doors.
A rolling army of Xs on your cousin's house.
They seem sharper here.

•

*This monument was built by the Russians
when they conquered Austria in 1945.*

Conquered? They call it *Zusammenbruch,*
"the collapse." Like the inevitable
but tragic fall of an opera house.

•

In the Hundertwasser Museum, the floors dip
and curve like a Bavarian landscape.
The windows are circles.

You can sign the guest list.
After your name draw a triangle on top
of another. A symbol they might know.

•

What other Viennese Jewish artists
can you think of? Kafka, Mahler.
Was Freud an artist? Marx?

No, Marx was German. And Mendelssohn's
father converted, didn't he?
You are bragging.

Yes, but consider:
The decline of any civilization directly corresponds
to its mistreatment of its Jews.

●

It is spring. If nothing else, the forsythia are brave.
Skinheads smashed some gravestones at the Central Cemetery
again. Driving the dead deeper into the ground.

Back at the river, they build apartment houses
with the concentration of ants. All around,
streets show what's beneath them. Gray as soot.

●

On the Judenplatz, signs on lampposts
hang where synagogues stood.

You read somewhere that the residents
don't want the plaques attached to their homes.

The signs are so high,
they could be perches for crows.

●

But the Kurzweils left Austria one hundred years ago.
You are just another raspy tourist muttering
at the river. If the gulls see something familiar
in the shape of your face, they do not remark on it.

•

Spit on the gravel.
Spread your dirt around.

•

From the park behind Schönbrunn Palace,
you can see the whole city. The buildings
have no features.

Sometimes it is an act of defiance to walk.

Under your breath, repeat again,
for Leuger and Haider and anyone not listening,
"Jude Chai, Jude Chai, Jude Chai. Here in your sick,
scarred city, a Jew lives."

•

Remember the Spanish horses? Wrapped in leather,
their awkward tricks for the men in caps,
how they dug into the ground?

When they were done, they bowed to you.
It was a gesture even they must dimly understand.
Remember how their knees were thin as wrists?

Balthus, *The Window*

I've heard this one before.
Take your shirt off. And I sit
on the windowsill, my hand
in the air, where he's put it.
It's early to be leaning back
above the damp courtyard,
the thin street. I hate
the bows on these shoes.
Why does he turn my ankle
toward the door? Why is my
hand so small? *Now lean back.*
But the rail is rusty,
like a rotten bough.
Bits come off on my sleeve.
Lean back to where? And now
he's put my chemise back on,
mostly. *Wear this locket,*
tilt your head. When he isn't
dressing me or moving me,
he is chewing the brush.
The breeze is cold up my back.
I wish this skirt could rise. I wish
the air in here wasn't so musty.
I wish my father would come home
with a jar full of money so Mother
could send us all to school.
Can I take off my shoe? *No.*
Can I loosen my belt? *Yes.*
He looks thin. Have you been eating?
He doesn't answer. The window
looks up to the rooftops.
If I had eyes on my neck,
I could see the dog barking below.
What color is it? I imagine
a green dog, his breath
like brushstrokes in the air.

Before the Debate

Before the debate each man checks his watch
to make sure time is still moving.
Go forward! they say to their wrists,
and it works. Moments pass. They are
like schoolboys hoping their show-and-tell project
will not embarrass them in front of the class.

The cameramen check their cameras
and the sound men check the boom mikes.
The producers scream and point, and the wives
of the two men grind out smiles
from their seats in the front row.
Everyone knows how important this is.

I am waiting for my wife to come home
from a business trip. I turn on the porch light
and lie on her side of the bed to warm it for her.
As the debate begins, she walks through the door
and I gently lift from her shoulders
her briefcase, her coat, her shirt, her hair.

While the auditorium fills with noise and light,
we conduct our own debate:
she asks leading questions
and I respond with an ambitious proposal.
She counters with figures but I stand my ground.
We astound the pundits by coming to a solution.

They spend the rest of the evening
staring mutely at us while we wrestle
over the details of our new compromise.

The Other Leo Baeck

This optimism becomes a demand for the heroism of man, for his moral will
to struggle. It is an optimism which strives to realize morality in practice.
—"Faith in God"

I am trying to locate a figure who can say something
about heroism. He has examples to elucidate his point,

but as of yet he has no face. It is difficult
to find anyone capable of grandiose pronouncements,

especially now when heroism itself seems confined to cartoon
and conjecture. I might add that this is part of his point.

Let's recognize the absurdity of trying to say anything new
about such a construct in the first place. Nevertheless

he must believe in his message. Frankly, it's nothing without him.
And vice versa, of course. He is only a figure

through which I'm hoping to tell you about heroism,
and after he has performed his duties, I'll have no qualms

about disappearing him. His brief life itself might then
be called heroic, I suppose. If the message has its value.

Which I must believe. One must believe in the value
of one's message, even if that message is only your life.

He needs to be someone who can accept irony and yet see beyond it.
Because even if the idea of heroism is absurd and foolish,

acts of heroism are no less compelling for fitting into a construction.
For instance, there's the story of the shtetl boys conscripted

into the Russian army, who were thrown into a river for baptism
and refused to return to the surface. One can imagine them

holding hands under water, giving each other courage, and the slowly
dawning silence on the surface. The figure would know about countless

martyrs for various causes, and must be able to discuss them in moving
language. How, though? And how might that reflect on my figure's message?

The question is significant because I want to tell you about
the other Leo Baeck, the one from Moravia who died at Theresienstadt,

and whose name was listed on one of those documents
the Nazis kept for such purposes. It turns out that Eichmann

saw this list and, assuming the name belonged to the famous
Rabbi Leo Baeck from Berlin, stopped demanding his immediate execution.

You might know of the subsequent accomplishments of the Baeck from Berlin,
in particular his philanthropy and his theology of ethical optimism,

but even if you have read his biographies, you'd know nothing
of his Moravian namesake except for the happy accident of his name

and the timeliness of his death. The question is, is the Moravian Baeck
a hero because by dying, unlike so many others, he managed to save a life,

and the life of an important man besides? Is he any less heroic
if he did so without desiring it, without even knowing it? What is the policy here?

The figure would be able to put this all together to great effect
if he is drawn convincingly. If not, there's nothing. He might as well

be reporting on what sort of flower thrives on human ash.
This is why I must attempt this project in the first place.

Since learning the story I admit I have been quite incapable
of performing my normal duties. One occasionally has a need

to disseminate information despite the obvious futility of the exercise.
But what do you need to know about me? The figure

is much more important. Or his message, or story, or statement,
which one hopes will travel from biography, to myself,

to the figure, and eventually to those of you who read this.
It may even have some vague influence on the way you feel

or think about heroism as a concept. Which is something.

Riding the Eighteen

—Jerusalem, 1996

Few words. I'd like to think it's because it's 6:30
on Tuesday morning and no one yet remembers
how to speak. But we know what's at stake.

We've scanned the faces climbing the stairs,
checked for jewelry, pursed lips,
something to reassure. The new bus

has improved air conditioning, bright flyers on the walls.
It's cool inside, despite the closeness of bodies:
shaved neck, crooked kipah, the bulge of a woman's

back above her bra. As we roll towards Talpiyyot,
the crowd thins out. A metal statue of two goats
like a weathervane always facing east.

Two synagogues on one triangular lot.
On descent, there's a release,
but also something like disappointment:

giving up the post, once again no part of history.
The bus pulls off with its rank exhaust
trailing it like a memory of violence.

Night Driving

No one selling cherries

                at roadside kiosks,

no whitetails chewing

                gravel, forelegs pointed

at the guardrail.

                Minivans kick up

what's left of the rain,

                passing. Yellow

divider uneven, slanted.

                Engine a conch shell.

We are headed north

                at a speed familiar to baseballs.

Trees hiss with crickets

                or wind, flash

brights at oncoming trucks

                to warn them of speed traps. She sleeps

curled against the window,

                her prerogative

after our snarls and whispers.

                We lean left,

I right us. She doesn't stir

                as we rush over a bridge,

the rumble of the road

                suddenly a Gregorian chant. If I turn

the wheel two inches, this

                argument will be over.

                          Two inches.

Conciliatory Letter to Morgan

Enclosed is the crushed ice I have promised you.

Last night a few of us jolted the mirrors loose at the Mineshaft,
our teeth glowing in the blue light like deepwater fish.
Shirley was there, your smell in her hair and an obvious lie.
She said you were here and gone.

I know you keep doing this: buzz into town, biplane,
staying with her quiet like you're hiding from the fuzz,
then just when the detectives break down the door,
poof! Dust on the stereo, dust in the tea.
Your motives lucid as a cartoon thought balloon.

But it's me. Don't you remember our promises at the concrete court?
Your mustard artichokes, our hesitant tongues?
Remember the broken tooth, the towering tuxedo,
coconut milk boiling sweetly in a rusty wok ?
Where is the other half of the dollar, Morgan?
50,000 hubcaps and see if I wasn't right all along.

Oh, trying to say what I feel
is like sculpting with live spiders.

Morgan, forgive me. If this letter reeks of old anger,
if the paper is chintzy and the ink all splotched,
imagine me here on the roof of the library,
fabricated history of the known world shelved beneath my thighs.
Isn't there some message in this for us?
Can't you picture us in handstand,
slowly pushing it all back into the earth where it belongs?

Shylock Visits Dachau, 1991

Thou torturest me, Tubal. It was my turquoise; I had it of Leah when
I was a bachelor. I would not have given it for a wilderness of monkeys.

Shylock emerges from Brandenburg Gate blinking,
    as if under a spotlight.

Gypsy vendors sell chunks of the wall big enough
    to kill Abel. Never

has destruction been such an act of beauty.
    He passes through

slow and unnoticed, makes his way West
    thinking of Jessica

in Tel Aviv, aerograms in her tight script:
    I am still your daughter,

after all that has happened. Please answer
    so at least I know you are well.

People are selling televisions and toaster ovens
    by the gross on the platz. Young men

haggling, he pauses to listen, ears pricking up,
    hearing suddenly sharp,

then he continues his walk.
    His zlotys are not worth much here.

Still, there's always the possibility . . . but no,
    that's not why he has come.

He meets an old business associate at a chic café
    who will take him

to Munich. After that he's on his own.

•

Frankly, I never liked him. Always
arguing over prices and contracts even when
it became difficult to simply get materials that far east.

I was a distributor for Dresden porcelain until '33.
He was my contact in Lublin. When things started,
I told him, "Take your wife and daughter, and get out of here.

Take a boat to Sweden, or America." But he thought
he had enough money to keep the local kingpins satisfied.
He learned quickly enough when the kingpins

became local landmarks. They say one day
he took his daughter and left,
without a word to her, took everything.

I guess he figured they stood a better
chance without her. She was already ill. Turns out
she was stronger than he'd thought.

She lasted two years at Majdanek.
Then came the relocation.
I know this because I was a railway worker at the time,

a petty officer at Dachau.
When the Americans first arrived,
I lived in the stockade for a while,

but I was ranked too low to amount to much
and they let me return to Dresden,
such as it was. Later I received a letter from him,

postmarked Lublin. It was as if nothing
had changed for him. He was distributing glass again,
bribing the new tyrants. But now,

with the changes, and this country
open to the East like a long-lost rich uncle,
he can come to bury his wife. To ask forgiveness.

And if all he asks of me
is a ride to Munich, how can I refuse?
Even for a man like him.

•

He's exchanged enough marks for a hostel
on the outskirts, enough for apples and cheese
from a street vendor, enough also

for the commuter train to Dachau,
but he knows as well as anyone
you don't have to pay for the trains in Germany.

It's a short ride he takes standing,
eyeing the pretty American backpackers,
scratching his chin raw beneath his red beard.

He does have to shell out 3 DMs for the bus,
which rattles its way through suburban Dachau,
The pamphlet issued by the tourist's office reads:

"After your visit, you will be horror-stricken.
But we sincerely hope you will not
transfer your indignation to the ancient Bavarian

town of Dachau, which was not consulted
when the concentration camp was built."
Entrance to the memorial is free of charge.

A barbed-wire sculpture, twisted heads
and hands like badly drawn stars,
reminds him of nothing. He takes his walk

through the damp museum: perfunctory documents,
numbers, gold teeth on display in glass cases.
Outside, the whole compound is covered

with gravel. Only two barracks stand in the rain,
clean and desolate, the wood varnished. Tourists
whisper and point as they wander through

the well-kept grounds, eyes on their watches.
He barely sees the cleaned-out
crematorium, or the artful memorials.

He reinspects the photographs, but doesn't
find what he's looking for. Scanning the figures,
hollow faces darkened by shadow, he thinks,

"All this time I was wrong. I thought I'd find
the remnants of my anger, but there's nothing here.
Not even ghosts to trick my useless eyes."

•

When he returns to the bus kiosk, he has
        pocketed one of the thumb-sized
stones which keep the park unmuddied.
        He's got it with him

when he returns to Lublin and when
        he climbs the stairs
to his apartment, the familiar scratch
        of his shoes on the mat. He rests

it finally on a table where his daughter's
        letters lie strewn—opened,
face down—and the turquoise ring
        she returned to him,

and the photograph of the three of them
        in the ornate silver frame.
Leah's pursed smile reemerging, the black
        cloth finally removed.

Simcha

The men pogo into each other like wind-up toys,
complete with iron smiles.
It's a rough circle: they move in for a turn, snarl,
then shift outside
to watch and catch their breath. The groom
just got his second wind. Both knees in the air,
he's absorbed in his own movement, watching his feet stomp,
a whirling Buddha.
One man jumps in with his fedora aflame,
an old trick.
Another, payis slick and gleaming,
balances a wine bottle on his head,
runs circles, his eyes fixed on a space behind his eyes.
The band keeps pace, keyboard switching to clarinet,
then vocals:
 "Moshiach! Moshiach! Moshiach!" The joint is jumping.
Even the seventy-year-old rebbe
does yoyo tricks and reeks Scotch.
Even the clean-shaven relatives from the East
do the best they can. Work it.
Male sweat thick in the air.
They lift the groom again to see his bride on the other side—
this time without a chair.
Calves knotted, he stands on the balancer's shoulders.
His grin is furious, his kipah askew, tuxedo shirt
showing damp at the stomach.
With the height, he hovers above the amplifiers.
Across the divider, the women dance
a calmer hora, clap their hands with spread fingers.
She sits in the center, grinning at them.
It's so quiet where he is now, he can almost hear her dress shift,
the fabric stiff
under his fingers when he lifted her veil.
She looks up and sees him, her lipstick
smudged, her eyes wild
and striking. She closes her lips for a moment,
and he lets himself fall
back into the music, the riot, the sea of hands.

I Am Fortunate in a Memory of Sounds

Trains in the stockyard answer the piano
in its own whale-language,
not the noise I bang from its bones.
Wind makes bassoons of the eaves,
and distant traffic, a fading trumpet call,
ricochets off the rear wall. You are gone again, glissando.
You and your timpani laughter.

You have missed the weeks of gnat swarms on the porch,
the cardinals hawking their wares,
the light applause of spring rain on the roof.
Here crickets scratch out their mysteries
from perches in the vetch and bushes. Here an ambulance
blares down the street with its panicked cargo.
Here the absence of your hair sifts against my ear.

Come home. Bring shouts and cymbals,
bring feedback and terrible atonal accusations.
Bring silence. If cicadas
can drown out our neighbor's Labrador,
and radio static snap synapses for miles,
we may recompose ourselves. Let's begin
with your shoes dropping in the doorway.

Friday in Jerusalem

We wake to roosters arguing over tractates of Talmud.

Out on the street, boys invent new meanings for old
languages, the way they always have.
A woman scolds a driver: Keep that kid's
head in the car! What kind of father are you?

We pass last night's art fair on our way to the Old City—
Hezekiah's Wall erect in its pit, still defying the Assyrians.

The holy sites are quiet: everybody's
shopping. Later, at services, a woman leads
the evening prayers from a perch an octave above us.

We launch our voices. Behind, a simpleton
reverently raises his new watch to the ceiling.

Article of Faith

David: coming home from a film today, my brain
so zoned on a close-up of an actor's mouth and teeth
that I almost walked into a bus, I thought of you.
Only you could make me love L.A.,
you with your electric beard.
Years ago we poured ablutions of Ethiopian beer
over the feet of the Buddha;
we climbed concrete to a beach bonfire;
we sneered at Trader Vic's like upright citizens,
and I want to tell you that I am no longer as lost as I was.
I know when I saw you last I was counting slips
and the numbers weren't good.
I want things more than I want to want them.
You, though, were steadfast like a priest.
You were true like the word tries to be true.
I read in the paper about a pilot who veered
his crashing plane into the waves
to save whomever he thought
lived in an empty farmhouse he could see from the cockpit.
We need our fictions. And look:
your California coast shimmers with promises,
with mists and frigates;
and I am in possession of a goodly heritage,
a dynasty of defiance with acrostic martyrologies.
And yet despite our bruised students,
despite our shaky foundations
and everything we know about everything we know,
I still have this vague, wiry
belief growing in me like a cactus,
like acacia clinging to the crumbling soil.
You know about this—it's you who taught me.
I'm writing to tell you, David, that I accept, I accept it all.
Let the idols of apathy be multiplied,
I will not take their names upon my lips.
I am hefting my ideologies—with all their incumbent clichés—
and I am carrying them to California.

My friend, among the shards of our deconstruction
I believe there grows a kind of manna.
I am writing my way west to celebrate some old lies with you.

Psalm

We're late. She pulls on hose, as if her skin
were too sensitive for the air, and weaves

around the unmade bed, socks on the floor,
sweatpants failing to climb the desk chair.

She gathers papers, bumps me on my way
out of the bathroom, drops them, swears,

reshuffles, pecks my cheek to let me know
It's not you. 7:50. The service starts at eight.

I wait at the piano, play a tarantella.
The gray skirt suit broadens her shoulders,

very professional. Hair pulled back,
perfume subtle, earrings simple and elegant.

•

Most of the members only summer here: yachts
        on Lake Michigan.
In winter it's tough to get a minyan, but tonight,

there are not enough prayerbooks to go around.
        Maybe it's the new rabbi.
The rented Church hums with voices,

and someone opens the front door
        to let some air into the place.
I sit next to Mel Feldman as he shoos his senile wife

from the gold earrings of the woman in front of us,
        dangling like wind chimes.
Oh Sylvie. He grips her hand in her lap, grits his teeth.

From the front come the welcoming remarks, then:
       Let us rise for the Barchu.
Mrs. Klein does her best with the ancient upright,

and the congregation lifts its wobbly voice
       for the summons prayer,
once sung with ram's horns. *Praised be the Lord,*

to whom our praise is due, now and forever.
       The first of many redundancies.
The young rabbi arranges the kiddush cup while we sing.

Praise for the Lighter of Fire, praise for the One
       Whose Word Makes
Evening Fall. The same pattern every time.

Praise for the God of our Fathers: Abraham, Isaac,
       and Jacob. The rabbi adds:
And for our mothers: Sarah, Rebecca, Rachel and Leah.

The sermon is about bringing religion into our lives,
       and the rabbi performs it
with conviction, if not polish. She'd been revising it

until this afternoon. Final praise for the Source of Peace,
       for the One
Who Spread Out the Heavens and Established the Earth.

Whispers behind me: *That's the rabbi's husband.*
       Praise for Beverly Goldstick,
who is hosting the oneg. Praise for everyone who helped her bake.

After the closing song, I am congratulated by blue blazers
       and lace wrists, gray smiles,
penciled eyebrows. *You must be so proud.* Praise

for the gossip of widows and divorcées.
       Praise for their pleasure,
for their uncritical awe, praise for what keeps

a tiny congregation together: history, stubbornness,
    dues from downstate.
Praise for the woman who has led them tonight,

drifting now among plastic cups of grape juice
    with her trademark tired smile.
Praise for these my hands, which will hold her hips and back,

later, curtains drawn, when everyone is home and at rest.

Acknowledgments

Grateful acknowledgment is given to the following magazines, which published these poems, some in earlier versions:

Another Chicago Magazine: "The Merry Crew"
ARC: "Our Business is Rejoicing"
Chattahoochee Review: "Tacitus"
Connecticut Review: "Burying Carnations"
Crazyhorse: "Jew in a New Suit"
Farmer's Market: "Night Driving"
Fiddlehead: "Song"
Greensboro Review: "Balthus, *The Window*"
Jewish Currents: "Bris"
Judaism: "Document," "Simcha"
Kairos: "Before the Debate"
The Kenyon Review: "Vienna March"
The Literary Review: "Forbidding Mourning"
The Malahat Review: "I Am Fortunate in a Memory of Sounds"
Parchment: "The Sacred and The Profane"
Poetry East: "Doctrine"
Prairie Schooner: "Variations on *Jonah*"
Response: "Shylock Visits Dachau, 1991"
River City: "'Blessed Is the One Who Releases Me from This
    Responsibility," "Life, McKenzie"
Sonora Review: "My Father's Hands"
Southern Poetry Review: "Poem"
Whiskey Island Magazine: "Thrash"

For "Shylock Visits Dachau, 1991," I am indebted to James E. Young's *The Texture of Memory: Holocaust Memorials and Meaning* (Yale University Press, 1993) for the text of the tourist pamphlet and for other facts about Dachau.

"The Merry Crew" is based on material from Mark Richard's novel *Fishboy* (Doubleday, 1993), and uses some phrases from Celan's *Last Poems* (North Point Press, 1986), translated by Katharine Washburn and Margret Guillemin.

Thanks go to Don Bogen, Don McKay, Roger Mitchell, and David Wojahn for all their help and guidance; to Tony Chemero, Chris Green, Vivé Griffith, Chris Hudson, Terry Kirts, Jeff McKenzie, Michael Matkin, Khaled Mattawa, Jim Murphy, and Terry Wisniewski for their insight and friendship; to my family, for their constant support; and to Yael, for all of the above and extra.

This book is dedicated to the memories of Abraham Sol and Albert Sydney.